Praise for Darren C. Demaree

"In Darren C. Demaree's *Got There: Poems on Vanishing*, the title implies arrival, but the poems are a journey, each one traveling to bring the speaker closer to rest, each one ending with a plea just to be. In a landscape full of war and fires and politics, as well as deer and family and Ohio, Demaree uses repeated imagery respun into new matter, looking for an escape hatch into joy. Challenging and of the moment, *Got There* leaves the reader feeling, along with the speaker, that 'too often we are strangers to our own telling.' "

– **Donna Vorreyer, author of *Unrivered***

" 'The world is seven / questions asked / seven different ways' in Darren C. Demaree's *Got There: Poems on Vanishing*. To get there — toward an answer, or toward a significant silence — Demaree invents a form which ends with a shifting refrain: 'Be time with me.' 'Be the first step away with me.' 'Be real salt with me.' The result is a linked series rife with uncertainties, absences, blooms, and burials. One feels compelled to sing each final refrain aloud, in harmony with other lost souls. Be known with me."

– **Erica Reid, author of *Ghost Man on Second***

"It hasn't happened often in my life, but it has happened enough for me to realize immediately whenever I'm holding something so well made that my hands can FEEL the craftsmanship down to their bones. The heft, the smooth surfaces, the perfect joints and connections—this is exactly what my mind and heart feel reading a Darren C. Demaree poem. And his new collection, *Got There: Poems on Vanishing*, is no exception to that truth. A slice of cake sitting perfectly on a plate, a heavy question hanging unanswered, a breath full of memories, the blue feathers on the belly of the world, the perfection of milk and honey and morning together—it's all here, right in reach and waiting to be consumed. As these poems, this poet, remind us page by page, 'Don't let your hunger / ruin the swallowing of this day.' Take this collection poem by poem, swallow, taste, savor before any of it vanishes."

– **Jack B. Bedell, author of *Ghost Forest*,**
**Poet Laureate of Louisiana 2017-2019**

" 'Vanishing is its own genre,' explains the speaker of Darren C. Demaree's newest collection, *Got There: Poems on Vanishing*, a stunning and scrupulous meditation on the infinite arrivals we make over the course of a life—the intimacies of our encounters with those we love, with beauty and tragedy, with the particular burdens of American living, and with our own imperfect thinking—as we hurtle in the direction of an unmistakable end, each day undone, and remade, by time, deliberation, instinct, feeling. 'I am where I want to be, alive / & gone, but still able to see / the places you'll be if you decide / to follow me,' the speaker furthers, articulating an appeal to paradox, a wise and generous phenomenon able to hold all possibilities at once, the speaker seen and unseen, remembered and misremembered, involved and not. And what are the fruits of this vanishing, of this exquisite and complicated genre? 'I found belief in building / something sustainable so that / I could sustain elsewhere,' an elsewhere that is these very poems, the speaker's careful, questioning, well-meaning '...heart leaving / such epic trails.' "

– **Susan L. Leary, author of** *Dressing the Bear*

"While William Bronk was writing his book of fourteen-line poems, *To Praise the Music*, he kept a copy of Shakespeare's sonnets by his bed. He said eventually he thought in their shape, in the inimitable rhythm of those little square miracles. Darren C. Demaree's *Got There: Poems on Vanishing* similarly changes the cadence of your thinking, feeling, and hearing. These poems partition sixteen lines into nine, six, one; they repeat Be, ghazal-like, as they accrete imperatives along with knee-buckling flourishes like 'Ruin comes from wanting glass / on top of more glass.' or 'I wanted to be the blue feathers / on the belly of the world.' Demaree cultivates a great capacity for surprise in a closed form, which is how you know poetry is working. He writes and writes these fraught silver rectangles, wracked with love and pain and American life. One poem implores, 'Let me begin again.' It's a permission gorgeously easy to grant."

– **Tom Snarsky, author of** *Reclaimed Water*

# GOT THERE:
## poems on vanishing

darren c. demaree

©2026 Darren C. Demaree
Cover ©2026 Robyn Leigh Lear
"ibid" ©2026 Alina Stefanescu

-First Edition

All rights reserved. No part of this publication may be reproduced or transmitted in any form or by any means, electronic or mechanical, including photocopy, recording, or any information storage or retrieval system, without permission in writing from the publisher.

Publisher's Cataloguing-in-Publication Data

Demaree, Darren C.
  Got there: Poems on vanishing / written by Darren C. Demaree
  ISBN: 978-1-953932-44-0

1. Poetry: General 2. Poetry: American - General I. Title
II. Author

Library of Congress Control Number: 2026933690

*This book is dedicated to my community of fellow poets. We speak in, around, and through the madness. Sometimes we even find each other.*

"ibid" by Alina Stefanescu

Author Statement

As an artist, your most valuable skill is a lithe heart and mind. Experiencing other artist's work, being affected by it, speaking to it, and allowing the confluence of both voices in a new expression is one of the more beautiful parts of being in and working within a community of artists. When Alina posted the photo "ibid" of a streetlight dancing and then disappearing before finally returning at the edge of frame, it stirred inside me my own desire to disappear, if only for a while, in pursuit of something more—a safer intimacy in this dangerous world. The friction of leaving but wanting to be seen was what made my study of the photo so generative. I'm thankful for Alina and her work. I'm thankful for this community I'm a part of— the only one beyond my family that I would never considering leaving.

## Contents

| | |
|---|---|
| Got There: Cake | 13 |
| Got There: Paw at It | 14 |
| Got There: A Common Definition of Beauty | 15 |
| Got There: Mournful | 16 |
| Got There: It's Never Going to Stop | 17 |
| Got There: A Western Idea of Triumph | 18 |
| Got There: Absolule Want | 19 |
| Got There: As an Animal | 20 |
| Got There: This Map | 21 |
| Got There: I've Written Worth | 22 |
| Got There: The Rock's Old Ribs | 23 |
| Got There: Metal Chains | 24 |
| Got There: Absence is Presence | 25 |
| Got There: It Would Be Better if I Had No Place to Hide | 26 |
| Got There: Warm and Cold Air | 27 |
| Got There: The Sea and Sky Bend | 28 |
| Got There: Shown Standing | 29 |
| Got There: Stone Talk | 30 |
| Got There: Loved Ones | 31 |
| Got There: Moving On | 32 |
| Got There: Paper Chains | 33 |
| Got There: On Beauty | 34 |
| Got There: Terrifying and Fearlessly Inventinve | 35 |
| Got There: Fat Door | 36 |
| Got There: The Hour Shifting | 37 |
| Got There: Collecting | 38 |
| Got There: I Dreamed of Me and You | 39 |
| Got There: The Seeds Employed | 40 |
| Got There: Burning | 41 |
| Got There: Burnt | 42 |

## Contents

| | |
|---|---|
| Got There Ash | 43 |
| Got There: Real Color | 44 |
| Got There: Earth Houses Rising | 45 |
| Got There: Patterns of Light | 46 |
| Got There: The Rate is Flat | 47 |
| Got There: So That I Believe It's Possible | 48 |
| Got There: Believe Me, Love | 49 |
| Got There: Not Speech or Gender | 50 |
| Got There: Stop | 51 |
| Got There: Slap the Water | 52 |
| Got There: Lands | 53 |
| Got There: Thousand Star Field | 54 |
| Got There: Twilight | 55 |
| Got There: I Was Inexplicably Happy | 56 |
| Got There: Wading Naked | 57 |
| Got There: Adoration | 58 |
| Got There: An Indefinite Series of Rivers Ending at Our Feet | 59 |
| Got There: The End | 60 |
| Got There: It Makes Sense During the Day, It Makes Sense at Night | 61 |
| Got There: If There is an Asking Price | 62 |
| Got There: One Thing Raised over My Head | 63 |
| Got There: Peace or Quiet | 64 |
| Got There: Rest | 65 |
| Got There: The Symmetry of Being Alone | 66 |
| Acknowledgments | 69 |
| About the Author | 71 |

Darren C. Demaree

Got There: Cake

Sugar cannot be misshapen.
The crystal orchard holds
no knowledge, only beauty
& a spoon. Warm by the old
fires, dare you dream about
the times you turned down
a layered cake when offered?
It shimmers because it comes
from a place that abhors secrets.

There are no secrets. What if
I showed you a plate
that was empty because
it never held anything at all?
Look down at your hands.
Sugar cannot be misshapen.

Be whole & simple with me.

**Got There: Poems on Vanishing**

Got There: Paw at It

That moment comes along
where it feels like there can
be no more play, where you turn
your lack of the infinite
into a very serious thing
that must be reckoned with,
that because this place is living
& that means dying, telling jokes
to birds is a waste of time.

It's the pain that has your attention.
You want to hold something else.
Lithe-hearted ones, you can't strip
joy from the riverbanks.
Please, turn down every offer
to keep any part of this world.

Be free of weight with me.

**Darren C. Demaree**

Got There: A Common Definition of Beauty

The world is seven
questions asked
seven different ways
& an overexcited
silence that builds
towards earthquake
or religion or a crop
raised to be burned
by our confusion.

Let not knowing
be the gentle wave
it can be. Give apples
to a young hunger.
Look back. Call it
looking forward.

Be simple with me.

# Got There: Poems on Vanishing

## Got There: Mournful

Dear robes,
I assumed
the glory
of seven years
spent leaving
& all I looked
was lost.
Life into death.
Life into death.

I lived on
the porch
so the field
could feel me
coming. Crop
didn't care.

Be time with me.

**Darren C. Demaree**

Got There: It's Never Going to Stop

How brazen, for a whole world
to look away from the waters
& to be more playful with burials
than birthing rituals, for births
to become the first consideration
of the body-count, of the layering
of the bodies beneath the electric
lamp. Is this the first ugliness?

I put my four fingers on the chin
of the named weight of organized
chaos & it offered to keep me
tucked in a cheek. It was a dry
throat sort of love. I turned away
& I never needed to turn again.

Be the first step away with me.

**Got There: Poems on Vanishing**

Got There: A Western Idea of Triumph

According to the text,
which means according
to the pangs of hunger
& lust, we are all meant
to leave home with
an ugliness that defines
us. I refused to leave
home, so my home left
me. Floods aren't subtle.

I followed the horses
when they went off
the cliff. I flew when
the horses flew. I died
when the horses died.
Our flesh draped poorly.

Be the old nature with me.

**Darren C. Demaree**

Got There: Absolute Want


Alone, with two
ankles in water
that can rise
to make me part
of any other
water, I search
for no other rules.
The nice tune
is almost silence.

All legends are dry
as old shit. Even
the owlets know
silks don't belong in
the river. Born apart,
I want questions.

Be uncertain with me.

**Got There: Poems on Vanishing**

Got There: As an Animal

Just be simple. Walk
away from the conceits.
Refuse all premises.
Noonday is for police
& church people.
Leave at night. Don't
stray from the waters.
If you find good sand,
write your philosophy.

Meanwhile, the skin
& the infinity will follow
you to the places
where nothing can be sold.
The field is broadminded.
The dancing is insightful.

Be moving with me.

Darren C. Demaree

Got There: This Map


Let's go to the pull
& worry, the kinky
vocabulary of death
as it promises climax
& delivers climax
& never quakes when
time glimpses back
for company & sees us
with frosted tongues.

I know I want to be
lost in the trees of land
nobody owns. I don't
want to be found, but I
want to tell everyone
where I'm going.

Be vanished with me.

**Got There: Poems on Vanishing**

Got There: I've Written Worth

There is no way to breathe
without breathing through
the dead. Let me begin again.
I'm an American, but I've never
wasted my love. I like to point out
that every golf course is a burial
ground, but I'll use the pool
next to the eighteenth. Pools are
where my children like to swim.

I want joy, but I cannot write it.
I want love, but I cannot love
myself. I want to leave the city
& still be seen from the highway
as you pass the new county signage.
I want to try in front of you.

Be with me from a great distance.

Darren C. Demaree

## Got There: The Rock's Old Ribs

I don't need to be
bricked in to hear
the silence of God.
Hell, I have a hammer
with me at all times
just in case a believer
tries to corner me
with a donation
from the deacons.

I cracked the rock
open to free the bats,
the fluttering hem
of the most important
cave. The ocean took
it away from me.

Be real salt with me.

**Got There: Poems on Vanishing**

Got There: Metal Chains

If you cannot
join me past
the fields,
where the trees
still stand up,
it's because
you haven't
noticed that
blood is yours.

Swim in it.
It will hurt.
The sounds
are the opposite
of music.
It's mining.

Be air with me.

Darren C. Demaree

Got There: Absence is Presence

Dear deceleration burial, the place
where the table used to be, winter
after the sprawl, the collapsing
collective, where we once built
communities because we loved songs
birds would sing near the riverside,
what is your plan for me, now that
you have me? How gentle will your ice
be as it navigates my final mass?

I don't have forty words for a single thing
in this world. I do know the exact phrases
to use for the sharpness I feel when I break
a chicken bone against my thigh
because I need a blade to take a politician
hostage because today is Thursday.

Be a dense, fleeting language with me.

**Got There: Poems on Vanishing**

Got There: It Would Be Better if I Had No Place to Hide

The nature of light is misleading. It's all fire,
flame or no. The smoky walls are unworried
& are conditional. The body suffers. Ugly is
an advertisement for art to do better
with the smell of things. Beauty is a promise
that things will never get better. I tell two lies
& a purple silk appears. The curtains are cute.
Upgather the gradient of this world
with a story of the divine. Lock the ending?

The cement path is a trap. I am on the lines.
I'm on each side of the lines. Clearly,
you're distracted by the lights. I want to find
something other than myself, but all these
questions are about me. Everything modern
hides. The custodians can only sterilize.

Be something better reaching back with me.

**Darren C. Demaree**

Got There: Warm and Cold Air

Ribbons is a kinder, more playful
name for the tethers we've been
cutting loose. Look at how they dance
in front of those angry faces
that do not listen when we tell them
here is the cool water, warmed
by the air that travels, that does not
care about the names of places.
Naming is such a terribly calm violence.

Our skin cannot feel the larger map.
Run side by side into the tree-line.
Only the bombers can kiss angry
enough to chase us from there
& their governments have gone
broke turning us all into fractions.

Be with me as we burn the boats.

# Got There: Poems on Vanishing

## Got There: The Sea and Sky Bend

I always wanted
to be with
the mess
completely
& to make lists
of beauty
that can drop
through the page
& pool to follow.

I am not with
the explanation.
I am with you.
A home in a head
& a heart leaving
such epic trails.

Be sticky with me.

**Darren C. Demaree**

Got There: Shown Standing

The storms are constant
& the water rises. I am
with the water. I am
with the deer corpses
that surround the water.
I am not with the smoke
or the wasting tides
of humanity. I'm tender
with death's four graces.

There has been too much
burial, too much un-
earthing the dead as well
& I'm tired of innovation.
Can you see me, unwilling
& tall in the contrasts?

Be tight fists with me.

**Got There: Poems on Vanishing**

Got There: Stone Talk

A skull is a stone
if you're not dragging
your fingers along
the jawline, if you're not
willing to be cut
by the true account
of our sharp history.
Too often we are strangers
to our own telling.

I don't know if I want
to be found now, away
from the people that know
my real names, or then
when you have to gather
my angles in the sun.

Be in the question with me

**Darren C. Demaree**

Got There: Loved Ones

The blood on our hands
is shared blood. The cold
odes stay cold. Believe
me when I tell you that
only my love could end
me, that only my loves
have tried to end me
& I would have it
no other way.

I'm vulnerable here, as in
I'm open, accepting
of each of their desperate
attempts to frame us
as something whole. They
never ask me questions.

Be the answer with me.

**Got There: Poems on Vanishing**

Got There: Moving On

To be away, finally, truly, but to keep
your hands closed; fist held firm to rot
& tighten against the wind is an absolute
waste. There are a thousand stars
& none of them are ours. Hallelujah!
None of them are ours! The unfamiliar
touches us to tease us into being born
again. Reality is as simple as an apple
without skin. We are for the elements.

When I was younger, when all my friends
were alive, when I was drunk all the time,
very, very drunk, all the time, I promised
a stranger I would write a poem in Paris
about basements in Ohio. It was a request
so beautifully strange, but I ignored it.

Be as beautiful as snow melting with me.

**Darren C. Demaree**

Got There: Paper Chains

*I have an offer for you.*
*I've made up an offer.*
*I've dreamt of a reward*
*for any that take my offer.*
*I've drawn faces on my dreams,*
*faces that look like your face*
*because your face is my dream,*
*owning your face is a dream*
*I've been told is very real.*

That is the same song that got
my grandfather, my father
& got me as well. The offer
is generational. The offer
gives you generations. Please
let my children sing of birds.

Be nothing at all with me.

**Got There: Poems on Vanishing**

Got There: On Beauty

I have trouble pushing past the idea
that the deer are everything.
They show up in my back yard
as ravine deer. They show up
in my front yard as city deer.
I've been trained to drive carefully
in every season Ohio imitates
& I mourn the one I hit driving
back to college on State Route 3.

All flesh loses heat in winter
when it pauses near the river
to watch a whole family cross
the water on an early morning walk.
We get to walk in the forest like we
belong here! We don't, really.

Be in the steam as it rises with me.

Darren C. Demaree

## Got There: Terrifying and Fearlessly Inventive

The ruin is an ode. The racism is a damn bone. A nation
can only be a tomb. The symbol of war is a hotel left
standing next to a bombed hospital. The symbol of war
is any government that can stockpile anything at all.
You have to split the tree before you can kiss splinters.
Who decided to split the tree? Who decided on hurt?
Whipped, curbed, parceled out, parceled in, this world
gave us love & we made an industry out of it, industry
only knows gears, gears only know other gears, blood
is oil in a factory. Trust the smoke only if it can disappear.

The ritual is a border. I want to lose the declarative
& return to a world of questions. All we are can stare
back at us. We must refuse that. The significance can
only return if we decide to be natural & true, if we lose
willingly, if we let the invitations lapse, if we let the world
close to us. I can be left. I can be left & sing anyway.

Be the account of something other than human with me.

**Got There: Poems on Vanishing**

Got There: Fat Door

A gift left in a basket to be
removed from the basket
is too much ceremony for me.
I want to hand you what
I have. It's not enough
that I will drop it from the idea
to the exchange. I want to carry
something for you. Let the debris
of my attention make promises.

There are bushes in front
of our house that used to be
burned twice a year. There's no
way it was legal, but that's what
they did. We planted mint
& refused to set another fire.

Be too much mint with me.

Darren C. Demaree

Got There: The Hour Shifting

What kind of courage is clean
enough to go at the world all over
again? I've seen time saunter
behind the bar with three knives
in an apron, waiting for me to be
brave, to order anything that takes
more than two fingers to make
& I drank every cheap beer
that I never wanted to see again.

Shame isn't much more than sharp
narrative held on to too tightly
by a person that's already bleeding.
If we choose to remember the meal,
what we ordered when we had a choice,
when joy was in our mouths, then?

Be away from the table with me.

**Got There: Poems on Vanishing**

Got There: Collecting

The fire is so damn
beautiful once it leaves
the trees. These gods
I keep hearing about, do
they really ask you to list
nineteen kitchen appliances
at the gates of wherever?
I bet we can go on living
without subscriptions.

Don't let your hunger
ruin the swallowing
of this day. If your hands
are free & moving
any moment can burst
into joyful smithereens.

Be light & lost with me.

Darren C. Demaree

Got There: I Dreamed of Me & You


I know work, the change of it,
the exchange of it, the thievery
& invented problems of work
& I know in the back of my mind
I am solving a work problem
right now. God dammit. All work,
even the best work, saving work,
in an economy, is a body floating
down a river towards a pile.

There are times when we forget
to breathe. We remember or we
remember. It will be okay in
the garden if we forget about
the garden. Put your hand in
your hand. Listen. I'll do the same.

Be the mind floating with me.

# Got There: Poems on Vanishing

## Got There: The Seeds Employed

I'm disturbed by how
much furniture there is
at my job. I don't want
to relax there. I know
what capitalism is, god-
dammit, you want me
to let my guard down
amidst the blood in
the snow of this world?

I've been tucked away
& told I'm crop. They
aren't subtle. Neither am I.
I asked the boss of my boss
to see if my life could fit in
their mouths. Cowards.

Be the sprawl with me.

Darren C. Demaree

Got There: Burning

Dazzling meteors
that we all are,
concessions made
to the predetermined
end of this planet,
a dagger stuck
between the breasts
of the previous beasts,
can we ask, why?

The all-genre is here
& it's smoke-jumping.
Let's fight the urge
to formalize it. Let's
lament the veil only if
we have to wear it.

Be coughing with me.

**Got There: Poems on Vanishing**

Got There: Burnt

Since the world
is no longer just
about the rivers
& ugliness is born
mostly in the fires
of greed or white
fear, escape takes
a triumph of tethers
torqued to loosen.

I used to be pretty
& then I was born
into the adult world
of death threats
for counting bodies
& knowing faces.

Be known with me.

Darren C. Demaree

Got There: Ash

The war is in two places. The war is in the heaven
in your mind. The war is in your hands. You
don't want the war, but the war is always there
& that horrible energy is so broad & squat
& predictable that the only thing you can believe
is that the war must be won. Such yellowish fang
this world can be if you're reaching past the chin
of your neighbors. Remember, if you're reading
this, the scarf is already around your throat.

I am not so glad that the fires happened, but seeing
that nothing but a thought can ever disappear
gives me hope that some of my worst thoughts
could disappear as well. It makes me think that if
I empty my hands, if I keep my mind clear of gods,
then I can look across the field and see no death.

Be warm and separate and remembered with me.

**Got There: Poems on Vanishing**

Got There: Real Color

I have heard the refrain of goals
& endings & burials of the burst
& I've gazed upon the great works
that have never ended hunger,
that have never taken away oxygen
from the rich & warring minority
& I must ask, is all this gray area
a white compromise? If it can't be
the sun, then we must set the fires.

I am not opposed to an ugly ending.
I'm outraged by anyone who claims
a new beginning. It's all happened.
It's all still happening. The fight
is to know it all, to wake up known
& knowing, to hue the witness.

Be early in the morning with me.

Darren C. Demaree

## Got There: Earth Houses Rising

Those new to dying stay
bathed in the world that
invited them to die at the end
of the same song that invited
them to live. How deeply does
the tree love us back? Could
we be brave enough to earn such
a love by freely giving our waters
back to the first, green note?

All these great men who never
stop talking like to ask me
for more, to do more, to make
more, to make myself more,
to say my name like it's more
than five syllables. Why?

Be given away with me.

# Got There: Poems on Vanishing

## Got There: Patterns of Light

Every time the temperature drops,
a moron is born. Morons
are the worst dancers in the world.
Their hips are locked. God curses
with both hands. I stay by the first-
floor window, listening to music,
ignoring the misinterpretations, I sing
the nonsense that makes me whole
& I dance well, with brazen knowing.

The birch tree looks at the blood
in the snow without judgment.
They are totally different things,
but are they? Where are we
in the epic? Subtlety has vanished.
I'm awake in the afterword.

Be long in the last winter with me.

Darren C. Demaree

Got There: The Rate is Flat

Ruin comes from wanting glass
on top of more glass. The balance
is breakable all the time. The dead,
the love of the dead, the semi-
fictitious afterlife of the dead, it
all pools beneath the forgotten fight
of the living. Let the feasting fungi
tell our last story. Let the expense
be buried with us or let the crows win.

The larger object is just an object.
A thing stays a thing forever. We are
not things. We are space in time.
We are empty pockets. We are pockets.
The epic demands that every debt
is meaningless. Trust this fabric.

Be unable to pay the cost with me.

**Got There: Poems on Vanishing**

Got There: So That I Believe It's Possible

Hate & fear & all
those sleeping pills
the studies show
increase my lean
towards dementia,
but I still take out
of routine. The world
leaks. I cheat to sleep.
It's all pale yellow.

Whiteness rots first.
The electric lights
dance on naked walls.
I want nothing. I want
to be nothing. Nothing
is coming for me.

Be simple with me.

**Darren C. Demaree**

Got There: Believe Me, Love

Between up
& down, the poverty
of the dream
dreamt already, held
as an ending during
the mouthful
that is a life, that is two
lives speaking
only in questions.

Answers are capital
& we've had enough.
Which is to say
we are at war
with the unforgiving
shadow of worth.

Be silence with me.

**Got There: Poems on Vanishing**

Got There: Not Speech or Gender

The boil sprawls by the end of day
& each muscle that manages to cling
to each bone is a victory. We take
any adornment as a gift, but what if
every trophy is a trap? I can say
the living silence is how I want
to identify. I'm just not able to take
the idea of winning without shaking
loose every tongue of every coach.

The sparrow whips the wind for fun.
The blood passes no opportunity
to force the snow into becoming a ship.
A mind can get lost inside a body.
A name is a piece of equipment.
The bear's tongue cannot metaphor.

Be milk & cherry & morning with me.

**Darren C. Demaree**

Got There: Stop

I hold myself again. I hold myself
in the sparkling light that did not
have to exist, but it does in this
unbearable beauty I can finally see
separated from the context,
reflecting nothing but an existence
that began with screaming, goes
on now with even more screaming
& then what? We shouldn't be afraid.

Let's believe enough that this world
can exist without us so that it feels
like something other than chaos
when we go far enough into
the landscape that we become part
of the landscape. Paint me as a tree.

Be the second step away with me.

# Got There: Poems on Vanishing

## Got There: Slap the Water

What can we learn from all these
dead flowers, if not the courage
to smell the beautiful decay
of what was once so filled with
water's kiss? This world is folding
into itself. The water is retreating
& all we can think about is waves.
We have such flat, angry hands
built to violently spill this time.

There should be more hobbyists
obsessed with the linguistic
associations of the honey that
refuses to become a bee balm
that cannot be flavored with cherry
because it's never, ever been held.

Be the bloom retreating with me.

Darren C. Demaree

Got There: Lands

I own nothing.
I own nothing.
I own nothing.
I own nothing.
I own nothing.
I own nothing.
I own nothing.
I own nothing.
I own nothing.

I own nothing.
I own nothing.
I own nothing.
I own nothing.
I own nothing.
I own nothing.

Be with me.

**Got There: Poems on Vanishing**

Got There: Thousand Star Field

There is too much
armor. There are
too many motors.
The true accounts
of the birds have been
turned into metaphor.
Milky & desperate,
our eyes spasm in
the sun, they fog fear.

Forget arriving, move
into the field, wait
for the living blanket
to remove your names.
Let those people in black
machines tear past you.

Be revealed with me.

**Darren C. Demaree**

Got There: Twilight

So much of being an adult
is being seen. I don't want a presence.
I don't want to plunder. I don't
want to be part of any construction.
I don't want to be made in the image
of a god. I don't want the rivers
to pass me & I don't want to
drown outside of the rivers.
I don't want to miss the deer.

I want to stand next to my children
in front of the moon and lose all
doubt in the possibility of real joy.
I want to vanish with them
& be whole. I want to be taken
up by the distance of the stars.

Be runneled by the moon with me.

**Got There: Poems on Vanishing**

Got There: I Was Inexplicably Happy

I wanted to be the blue feathers
on the belly of the world. It took
me a long time to frame this all
as a bird that could fly, that could
sing, that could be seen as beautiful
as it hovered over us in a stream
we could breathe in. To be a color
& be kept, kept warm, kept away
to be nested, that was my dream.

The table was set before we arrived.
We were given a table! The open
air turned to song when love was
introduced. The birds flew beautifully,
colorful because sight desires a kiss
the same way a meal requires hunger.

Be loud and full in the trees with me.

Darren C. Demaree

Got There: Wading Naked

Everything was clear
when I was a body moving
with no other bodies.
I found belief in building
something sustainable so that
I could sustain elsewhere.
All my morning songs
were aggressive. I liked that
about me, my strong hope.

I took those flashes of joy
with the blood in the snow
& the late summer odes
& let the melodrama cook
in the plastic wrapper
we've gifted to everything.

Be after midnight with me.

## Got There: Poems on Vanishing

### Got There: Adoration

The gore used to be
an intimacy. Now, the utmost
is a firefly in an eclipse.
Now, the blood drips
through the letters of a name
& holy is the unspoken
feeder of the abandoned.
Does wanting to be seen
make you ugly? Does it?

Naming is a finger
dragged along the chin
of the colonial enthusiast.
There could be actual love
in the silent mannerism
of a hand blindly extended.

Be nameless with me.

Darren C. Demaree

## Got There: An Indefinite Series of Rivers Ending at Our Feet

Yes, the world is all old, tight knots
& the world is run by knot-makers
& rope-titans, determined to choke us
just enough that we can feel the real
pleasure of gifts we were already given.
*Unwrap this world we've kept barely
breathing!* Those fuckers changed rain.
They had only one idea, that our bodies
are separate, so they tried to bury us apart.

Pick a body of water. Follow it through
the county, into the city, past the suburbs
& into the field parties, ignore retention
ponds, breathe where no one watches
you breathe. You'll still feel the twine
tighten, but you'll be so close to me then.

Be at the end of all tethers with me.

# Got There: Poems on Vanishing

## Got There: The End

The milkweed is being
eaten. The short & tall
explanation of it
is all of us have mouths
& so few of us can
comfortably close them.
The social confession
lives in the throat. We
choke for each other?

A body is three songs
playing at the same time
& an army of crows
refusing to listen
to any of them, cawing
nonsense in return.

Be insistent with me.

**Darren C. Demaree**

Got There: It Makes Sense During the Day,
It Makes Sense at Night

The authentic world is a forest. The rest of it is
writing. Too many people consider the burning
of writing to be writing as well. Those fires yell
the strangeness, the cost, the money, the worst
of creation & the end of escape. Escape used to
be perfect. The forest used to be perfect. The cliff
calls & we hear a bank & so we jump off the cliff
like we've never felt anything at all. Eight fingers
turned against the thumbs, the deer reject us all.

Strangling isn't struggling. The layering of phone
messages is our later summer odes. The smirks
are a promise to abandon. I like to be naked
in the city. It's the only way I can perform being
owed, never owning, in front of this house
my wife bought. We, all of us, could leave today.

Be finally, finally fighting nothing at all with me.

**Got There: Poems on Vanishing**

Got There: If There Is an Asking Price

I put my mouth on the earth
& believed I was taking each
breath heart-first. It was lovely
& ruinous. Those with lungs
scattered my back among
the encroaching pavilions
& turned my tethers into song
& never pronounced my name
correctly. It was a true death.

Each bird is a hotel for flesh
found in the city. I got to live
in flight! I tell you I tasted death
as much as it tasted me. Gasp
if you must, but I was a part
of edges as they were eclipsed.

Be hidden in hope with me.

**Darren C. Demaree**

Got There: One Thing Raised over My Head

Nine trees & one stone pillar
in the background, all the water
gone, I am happy there are no more
trade routes, but I have one thing
left to sell. I have these shoulders
I've built up through nonsense
& fear & vanity & in pursuit
of easy pleasure & now that I am
only the distance, an invitation?

You can see me from where
you are. Can you make your way
to me? The wolves are eating.
The birds are taunting everyone.
I want to lift you up until I fail.
I want to fall for a god damn reason.

Be weak at the end with me.

## Got There: Poems on Vanishing

Got There: Peace or Quiet

Vanishing is its own genre.
The idea of the mark being
on the body, on attempting
to leave the body but still
be called flesh is an owl
in the morning, hunting frost.
The beauty comes from feeling
& the loss of feeling. The rush
of a needless flight matters.

Yes, I want the same as you.
I want my name to be said
out loud, but I have no interest
in being there when it's said.
If you are brave enough to say
I wrote this poem, thank you.

Be what happened last with me.

**Darren C. Demaree**

Got There: Rest


I can see the stars. I can see
the city. I can see where the road
gave way to the path which gave
way to me as I kept moving
towards the vanishing point.
I am where I want to be, alive
& gone, but still able to see
the places you'll be if you decide
to follow me. Bless this nature.

I've always wanted humanity
to be a pleasant fruit; to be skin
& seed, to smell sweet briefly
& to know the rotting is a gift.
It isn't & they don't, but now
I miss those trying witnesses.

Be away away away with me.

**Got There: Poems on Vanishing**

Got There: The Symmetry of Being Alone

Spiritually, I'm ill-suited for a chorus,
but I do love a rising action, I love
the color's preference for bright
& black, I loved being seen
from the angles I don't believe in.
The horizon clears, I'm alone
& I still exist, that is enough for me.
I get to be the plump fruit, rotting.

I refuse the premise of the sinner,
but I want the witness, I want
the testimony, I want the narrative
of my arrival and my departure.
I want the questions. I want them
to be answered by someone else.

Be the person who knows I'm gone.

## Acknowledgments

"Got There: On Beauty" – Apricity Press
"Got There: The End" – *Trampoline*
"Got There: Warm and Cold Air" – *Roanoke Review*
"Got There: Loved Ones" - Apricity Press
"Got There: Absence is Presence" - *Eunoia*
"Got There: The Rate is Flat" - *Eunoia*
"Got There: I Dreamed of Me & You" - *Eunoia*
"Got There: The Symmetry of Being Alone" - *Eunoia*
"Got There: Mournful" - *Eunoia*
"Got There: Lands" - *Eunoia*
"Got There: An Indefinite Series of Rivers Ending at Our Feet" - *COMP*
"Got There: A Common Definition of Beauty" – *COMP*
"Got There: Metal Chains" – *The Field Guide Magazine*
"Got There: Peace or Quiet" – *Chantarelle's Notebook*
"Got There: It Would Be Better if I had No Place to Hide" – *Chantarelle's Notebook*
"Got There: Real Color" – *Chantarelle's Notebook*
"Got There: Adoration" – *Version 9*
"Got There: Paw at It" – *Version 9*
"Got There: One Thing Raised Over My Head" – *Version 9*
"Got There: Wading Naked" – *pioneertown*

**Darren C. Demaree** grew up in Mount Vernon, Ohio. He is a graduate of the College of Wooster, Miami University, and Kent State University. He is the recipient of a Greater Columbus Arts Council Grant, an Ohio Arts Council Individual Excellence Award, the Louise Bogan Award from Trio House Press, and the Nancy Dew Taylor Award from *Emrys Journal*. He is the Editor-in-Chief of the Best of the Net Anthology and Managing Editor of Ovenbird Poetry. He is currently working in the Columbus Metropolitan Library system, and living in Columbus, Ohio with his wife and children. *Got There: Poems on Vanishing* is his twenty-fifth full-length collection of poetry.

## Similar April Gloaming Titles

*in defense of the goat that continues to wander towards the certain doom of the cliff*
Darren C. Demaree

*clawing at the grounded moon*
Darren C. Demaree

*Coming into an Inheritance*
Jeff Hardin

*V Verse Is I*
Jason Adam Sheets

*Dear Excavator*
Evan D. Williams

*What Haunts Me*
Bernadette Geyer

APRIL GLOAMING

View our full catalogue at aprilgloaming.com

www.ingramcontent.com/pod-product-compliance
Lightning Source LLC
LaVergne TN
LVHW031614060526
838201LV00065B/4835